1/2

Biodiversity

of Rivers

GREG PYERS

 **Marshall Cavendish**
Benchmark
New York

This edition first published in 2012 in the United States of America by
MARSHALL CAVENDISH BENCHMARK
An imprint of Marshall Cavendish Corporation

Website: www.marshallcavendish.us

This publication represents the opinions and views of the author based on Greg Pyer's personal experience, knowledge, and research. The information in this book serves as a general guide only. The author and publisher have used their best efforts in preparing this book and disclaim liability rising directly and indirectly from the use and application of this book.

Other Marshall Cavendish Offices:
Marshall Cavendish International (Asia) Private Limited, 1 New Industrial Road, Singapore 536196 • Marshall Cavendish International (Thailand) Co Ltd. 253 Asoke, 12th Flr, Sukhumvit 21 Road, Klongtoey Nua, Wattana, Bangkok 10110, Thailand • Marshall Cavendish (Malaysia) Sdn Bhd, Times Subang, Lot 46, Subang Hi-Tech Industrial Park, Batu Tiga, 40000 Shah Alam, Selangor Darul Ehsan, Malaysia

Marshall Cavendish is a trademark of Times Publishing Limited

All websites were available and accurate when this book was sent to press.

Library of Congress Cataloging-in-Publication Data

Pyers, Greg.
    Biodiversity of rivers / Greg Pyers.
        p. cm. — (Biodiversity)
    Includes index.
    Summary: "Discusses the variety of living things in the ecosystem of a
river"—Provided by publisher.
    ISBN 978-1-60870-531-3
    1. Rivers—Juvenile literature. 2. Freshwater biodiversity—Juvenile literature.
    3. Stream ecology—Juvenile literature. 4. Endangered ecosystems—Juvenile literature. I. Title.
    QH97.P94 2012
    577.6'4—dc22

                                                                    2010037463

First published in 2011 by
MACMILLAN EDUCATION AUSTRALIA PTY LTD
15–19 Claremont Street, South Yarra 3141

Visit our website at www.macmillan.com.au or go directly to www.macmillanlibrary.com.au

Associated companies and representatives throughout the world.

Copyright © Macmillan Publishers Australia 2011

Publisher: Carmel Heron
Commissioning Editor: Niki Horin
Managing Editor: Vanessa Lanaway
Editor: Georgina Garner
Proofreader: Tim Clarke
Designer: Kerri Wilson
Page layout: Raul Diche
Photo researcher: Wendy Duncan (management: Debbie Gallagher)
Illustrator: Richard Morden
Production Controller: Vanessa Johnson

Printed in China

Acknowledgments
The author and publisher are grateful to the following for permission to reproduce copyright material:

Front cover photograph: Elephants crossing Mara river, Kenya courtesy of Nature Picture Library/Anup Shah.
Back cover photographs courtesy of Shutterstock/Eric Isselée (hippopotamus); Shutterstock/szefei (mountain stream).

Photographs courtesy of:
AAP Image/AFP, **14**, /Jaroslav Pap, **15**, /Wildlight/Bill Bachman, **25**; ANTPhoto.com.au/Gunther Schmida, **21**; Corbis/Martin Harvey, **27**, /JAI/Nigel Pavitt, **4**, /Sygma/John Van Hasselt, **23**; Dreamstime/Praveen Upadhyay, **28**; Getty Images/Gallo Images/Anthony Bannister, **10**, /Visuals Unlimited/Gary Meszaros, **18**; istockphoto/Patrick Gijsbers, **19**; Nature Picture Library/Dan Burton, **9** (left); photolibrary/Alamy/Alaska Stock LLC, **13**, /Alamy/Paul Mayall, **22**, /imagebroker.net/SWA SWA, **24**, /Science Photo Library/Planet Observer, **9** (right); Roland Seitre, **29**; Shutterstock/oksana.perkins, **16**, /John Sartin, **20**, /Dusan Zidar, **7**. Background images used throughout courtesy of Shutterstock/szefei (river), /TranceDrumer (waterfall).

While every care has been taken to trace and acknowledge copyright, the publisher tenders their apologies for any accidental infringement where copyright has proved untraceable. They would be pleased to come to a suitable arrangement with the rightful owner in each case.

Please note
At the time of printing, the Internet addresses appearing in this book were correct. Owing to the dynamic nature of the Internet, however, we cannot guarantee that all these addresses will remain correct.

1 3 5 6 4 2

Contents

Glossary Words

When a word is printed in **bold**, you can look up its meaning in the Glossary on page 31.

What Is Biodiversity?

Biodiversity, or biological diversity, describes the variety of living things in a particular place, in a particular **ecosystem**, or across the entire Earth.

Measuring Biodiversity

The biodiversity of a particular area is measured on three levels:

- **species** diversity, which is the number and variety of species in the area.
- genetic diversity, which is the variety of **genes** each species has. Genes determine the characteristics of different living things. A variety of genes within a species enables it to **adapt** to changes in its environment.
- ecosystem diversity, which is the variety of **habitats** in the area. A diverse ecosystem has many habitats within it.

Species Diversity

Species diversity changes from one habitat to another. Habitats such as coral reefs and rain forests have very high biodiversity. In the rain forests of Manu National Park in Peru, there are 1,300 butterfly species. This is far more than the total of 320 butterfly species found across the whole of Europe.

Habitats and Ecosystems

Rivers are habitats, which are places where plants and animals live. Within a river habitat, there are also many different types of smaller habitats, sometimes called microhabitats. Some river habitats are **estuaries** and **deltas**, and some microhabitats are the river bottom and the river edge. Different kinds of **organisms** live in these places. The animals, plants, other living things, nonliving things, and all the ways they affect each other make up a river ecosystem.

Both wildebeest and crocodiles are part of the biodiversity of the Mara River in Tanzania.

Biodiversity Under Threat

The variety of species on Earth is under threat. There are somewhere between 5 million and 30 million species on Earth. Most of these species are very small and hard to find, so only about 1.75 million species have been described and named. These are called known species.

Scientists estimate that as many as fifty species become **extinct** every day. Extinction is a natural process, but human activities have sped up the rate of extinction by up to one thousand times.

Known Species of Organisms on Earth

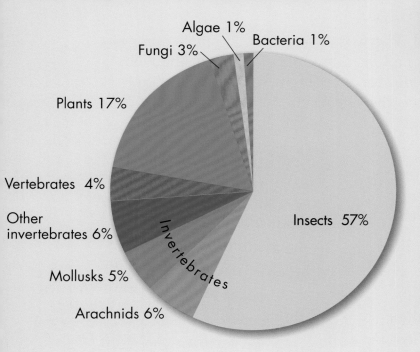

Algae 1%
Bacteria 1%
Fungi 3%
Plants 17%
Vertebrates 4%
Other invertebrates 6%
Mollusks 5%
Arachnids 6%
Insects 57%
Invertebrates

The known species of organisms on Earth can be divided into bacteria, **algae**, fungi, plant, and animal species. Animal species are further divided into vertebrates and invertebrates.

Approximate Numbers of Known Vertebrate Species

ANIMAL GROUP	KNOWN SPECIES
Fish	31,000
Birds	10,000
Reptiles	8,800
Amphibians	6,500
Mammals	5,500

Why Is Biodiversity Important?

Biodiversity is important for many reasons. The diverse organisms in an ecosystem take part in natural processes essential to the survival of all living things. Biodiversity produces food and medicine. It is also important to people's quality of life.

Natural Processes

Humans are part of many ecosystems. Our survival depends on the natural processes that go on in ecosystems. Through natural processes, air and water are cleaned, waste is decomposed, **nutrients** are recycled, and disease is kept under control. Natural processes depend on the organisms that live in the soil, on the plants that produce oxygen and absorb **carbon dioxide**, and on the organisms that break down dead plants and animals. When species of organisms become extinct, natural processes may stop working.

Food

We depend on biodiversity for our food. The world's major food plants are grains, vegetables, and fruits. These plants have all been bred from plants in the wild. Wild plants are important sources of genes for breeding new disease-resistant crops. When these plants become extinct, their genes are lost.

Medicine

About 40 percent of all prescription drugs come from chemicals that have been extracted from plants. Scientists discover new, useful plant chemicals every year. The United States National Cancer Institute discovered that 70 percent of plants found to have anticancer properties were rain forest plants. When plant species become extinct, the chemicals within them are lost forever. The lost chemicals might have been important in the making of new medicines.

Did You Know?

Mesopotamia is the name given to the ancient land between the Tigris and Euphrates rivers. About 9,000 years ago, humans used the plentiful fresh water and **fertile** soil in this area to first develop agriculture.

Quality of Life

Biodiversity is important to people's quality of life. Animals and plants inspire wonder. They are part of our **heritage**. For many people, a walk along a river is enjoyable because of all the wildlife that might be seen. Seeing a fish swimming in the shallows, a hawk soaring, or a lizard basking on a riverside rock are experiences that add interest and excitement to our lives.

Freshwater Fishing

Many people enjoy freshwater fishing with a rod and line. Each year in the United States, about 25.4 million anglers spend a total of 433.3 million days fishing in rivers and lakes. They spend $26.3 billion on the sport. This industry depends on healthy rivers that support a variety of fish species.

Walking beside a river and observing nature's biodiversity can enhance a person's quality of life.

Rivers of the World

Rivers begin in mountains or hills as tiny streams that join together to form larger and larger streams. The area of land that is drained by a river is called the catchment, or drainage basin. All the streams that join to make the river make up the river system.

The Course of a River

The course of a river is the path it takes from where it begins, called the source, to its end. The biodiversity of a river is affected by its changing course. The water in the upper sections of a river is usually cold, clear, low in nutrients, and fast flowing. It also has a high oxygen content, because cold water carries more oxygen than warm water. The river absorbs more oxygen as the water travels over rocks and rapids. It slows down as it moves over flat land, and it also picks up nutrients and **silt**. The water might also become warmer and slightly acidic.

The changing conditions create many habitats and affect the species biodiversity. Rainbow trout are unable to survive in water that is low in oxygen, so they live in parts of the river that have cold water, where oxygen levels are high.

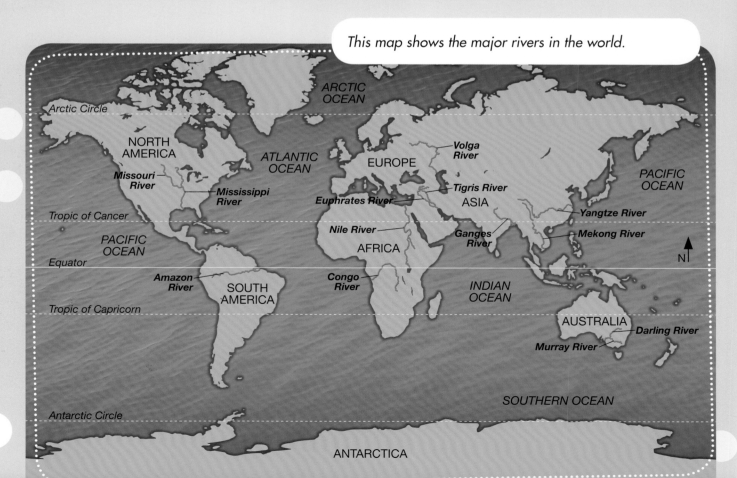

This map shows the major rivers in the world.

The Mouth of a River

Most rivers end at the sea or at a lake, or when they flow into a larger river. The place where a river meets the sea is called the river mouth.

Estuaries

Many rivers end in estuaries, which are sheltered bodies of water that empty into the sea. They are very important breeding places for many sea fish species.

Deltas

Some rivers end in deltas. These rivers carry a lot of silt, which they deposit at the river mouth, forming islands. The river itself divides into many separate channels that end at the sea. The islands support dense **vegetation**, such as mangroves, which are habitats for many animal species. There are many mudflats, too, which are rich in invertebrate life.

Seawater and river water meet and mix in estuaries.

This aerial view of the Nile Delta in Africa shows the triangular shape of the delta, where silt has been deposited.

Longest Rivers

CONTINENT	LONGEST RIVER SYSTEM	LENGTH (MILES)	CATCHMENT AREA (SQUARE MILES)
South America	Amazon	4,387	2,670,000
Africa	Nile	4,132	1,313,000
Asia	Yangtze	3,964	695,000
North America	Mississippi–Missouri	3,896	1,151,000
Australia	Murray–Darling	2,094	409,000
Europe	Volga	2,293	532,000

River Biodiversity

The biodiversity of a river includes the organisms found in the river and also the organisms found on the land alongside the river.

River Habitats

The biodiversity of a river is high when it has a wide variety of river habitats. Habitats in the river are the shallows, the mud of the river bottom, and the still waters of an oxbow lake. Other habitats are the habitats of the riparian zone.

The Riparian Zone

The riparian zone is the area where a river meets the land. It includes the river's edge, as well as the area of land that is affected by the river. The river provides this land with water and nutrients, which are deposited across the land when the river floods. The water and nutrients allow more plants to grow in the riparian zone than in the land beyond it. River red gum trees line the banks of Cooper Creek, an Australian desert river, but these trees do not survive in the desert beyond the riparian zone.

Mekong Fish Diversity

Southeast Asia's Mekong River has at least 1,200 species of freshwater fish. The Mekong giant catfish is the world's largest freshwater fish and can grow up to 10.5 feet (3.2 meters) in length and weigh up to 646 pounds (293 kilograms). The giant freshwater stingray grows up to 13 feet (4 m) wide, and the Siamese giant carp can weigh up to 660 pounds (300 kg).

The land along a river's edge has high plant biodiversity because of the water and nutrients that the river provides.

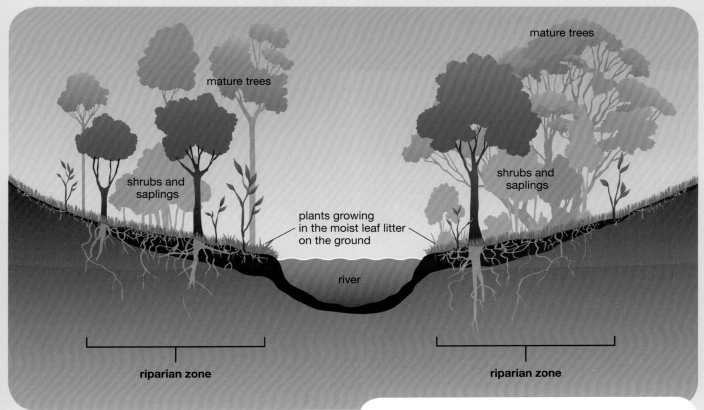

mature trees

mature trees

shrubs and saplings

shrubs and saplings

plants growing in the moist leaf litter on the ground

river

riparian zone

riparian zone

Many trees and plants grow in the riparian zone, because it is rich in nutrients and water.

Riparian Biodiversity

The riparian zone has rich biodiversity because it has many different habitats. It may have several layers of vegetation, such as:

- plants growing in the moist leaf litter on the ground
- a layer of shrubs and saplings
- an upper layer formed by the leaves and branches of mature trees.

These different layers attract different species of animals. Many of these species live only in the riparian zone. A study of a river flowing through a Canadian prairie found that there were up to seven times more bird species living in the riparian zone than in the surrounding grassland.

Did You Know?

The word *riparian* comes from the Latin word *ripa*, which means "riverbank."

River Ecosystems

Living and nonliving things, and the **interactions** between them, make up river ecosystems. Living things are plants and animals. Nonliving things are the rocks, soil, and water, as well as the **climate**.

Food Chains and Food Webs

A very important way that different species interact is by eating or consuming other species. This transfers energy and nutrients from one organism to another. A food chain illustrates this flow of energy, by showing what eats what. A food chain is easiest to understand in a diagram. A food web shows how many different food chains fit together.

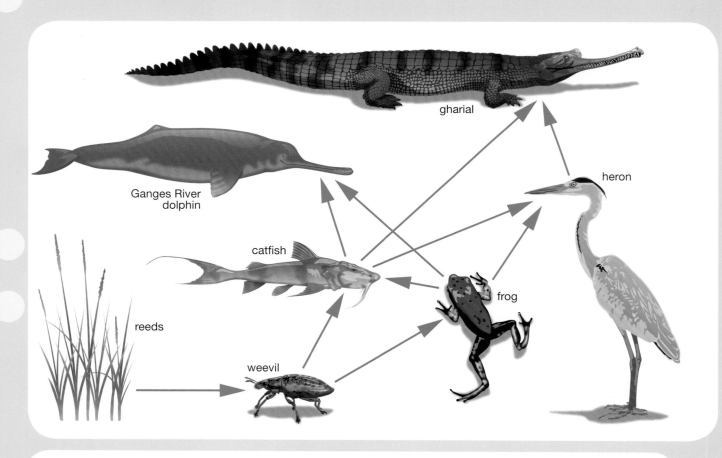

gharial

Ganges River dolphin

heron

catfish

frog

reeds

weevil

This Ganges River food web shows several food chains. In one food chain, reeds are eaten by weevils, which are eaten by frogs, which in turn are eaten by herons. Herons are eaten by gharials.

Other Interactions

Living and nonliving things in a river interact in other ways, too. Beavers build dams from rocks, mud, and trees that they cut down with their teeth. These dams form ponds or lakes in rivers, where the beavers can build their lodges, safe from **predators**. These ponds also provide habitats for other animals, such as young salmon. The salmon are safe from predators in the deep water, and they do not have to fight **currents** because the water is calm. The dam traps nutrients, which support the insects on which the salmon feed. The beavers create areas of open habitat for grazing animals, such as deer, when they clear the trees to make their dams.

Keystone Species

A keystone species is critical to the survival of many other species. The species may not have a large population, but its presence has a great influence on an ecosystem. The beaver is a keystone species because it transforms a section of river into **wetland**, creating habitats for wetland species that could not live there otherwise.

The North American beaver builds dams across streams and rivers, creating habitats for other species. Beavers are also found in some parts of Europe and Asia.

Threats to Rivers

Rivers around the world are under threat from a range of human activities. These activities change river habitats and ecosystems and threaten river biodiversity.

Biodiversity Hotspots

There are about thirty-four regions in the world that have been identified as biodiversity hotspots. These are regions with many **endemic species** where biodiversity is under severe threat from humans. Many of the world's biodiversity hotspots include rivers. The biodiversity hotspot of Sri Lanka and the Western Ghats of western India has 191 freshwater fish species in its rivers, and 139 of these are endemic species. More than 50 million people live in the area, and human activities such as farming and grazing are threatening the hotspot.

Human Threats

Some human activities that threaten to destroy river habitats and ecosystems are:

- animals grazing, which tramples vegetation and erodes the land in the riparian zone
- farming, which uses chemicals that can poison the water and land
- damming, which changes the natural course of a river and affects animal movements
- burning fossil fuels, such as coal and gas, which releases carbon dioxide into the atmosphere, causing climate change.

The Three Gorges Dam on the Yangtze River in China is the biggest dam in the world. Building the dam has destroyed the habitats of many species and the dam allows more ships to travel on the river, disturbing wildlife.

Mining Pollution

One disaster can destroy the biodiversity of a whole river, at least for a while. In 2000, a gold-mining reservoir collapsed and 3,531,000 cubic feet (100,000 cubic meters) of cyanide washed into eastern Europe's River Someş and, from there, into the River Tisza. Cyanide is an extremely poisonous chemical.

More than 331 tons (300 metric tons) of dead fish were removed from the river within days of the disaster. "The Tisza is dead," declared Serbia's Environment Minister. "Not even the bacteria have survived." However, one year later, the water quality of the river had improved, and some fish and birds had returned. Although some fish species had become quite rare, others had greatly increased in number.

Threats to Mussels

Mussels feed by filtering particles from water. This also helps to keep good water quality, which benefits other species in a river ecosystem, including humans. In the rivers of Oklahoma there are fifty-five species of freshwater mussels, but their numbers are declining. Pesticide pollution may be one cause. Pesticides are used to kill agricultural pests, but they can enter the river system and harm native species.

A volunteer removes poisoned fish from the River Tisza, in eastern Europe, after a mining accident spilled cyanide into the river in 2000.

BIODIVERSITY THREAT:
Urbanization

Most major inland cities have been built alongside rivers. Rivers provide water, which is necessary for human consumption and for industry. They are important transport routes, too. The main threats to biodiversity caused by **urbanization** are habitat destruction and pollution.

Habitat Destruction

Where a river flows through a city, riparian habitats have been replaced by roads, piers, and buildings. In many cities, creeks have been lined with concrete and stone, turning them into drains. The river bottom is sometimes dredged to make it deeper for boat traffic. This destruction of river habitats has severely reduced the biodiversity of city waterways.

Yangtze River Dolphin

The Yangtze river dolphin, or *baiji*, was declared extinct in 2006. It was found only in the Yangtze River in China. The construction of the enormous Three Gorges Dam reduced the dolphin's habitat, but other causes of its extinction were:

- loss of its prey, due to the destruction of its prey's habitat because of dredging
- noise pollution from river boats, which confused the dolphins and resulted in collisions with boats
- illegal hunting for its meat
- electric fishing, where an electric current is used to stun fish
- entanglement in fishing nets.

Tall city buildings line the edges of the Singapore River, in Singapore. The changed riparian habitat affects the river's biodiversity.

Pollution

Cities and towns are major sources of river pollution. Because the riparian zone has been altered, there is usually little or no riverside vegetation to trap **pollutants**.

For hundreds of years, rivers have also been regarded as convenient places to dump waste. The current carries the waste away downstream—for free.

Water Quality and River Invertebrates

The better the water quality in a river, the higher the number of invertebrate species, such as insects and freshwater crayfish. Invertebrate biodiversity is also higher where a riverbank is in its natural state. In one study, the water quality of the River Tame, which flows through Birmingham, in England, was found to be more important than riverside vegetation in producing high levels of invertebrate diversity.

Kinds of Pollution

TYPE OF POLLUTANT	SOURCES	EFFECTS ON BIODIVERSITY
Nutrients, especially nitrogen and phosphorus	Drains, **sewage** leaks, detergents, and fertilizer runoff from gardens	Algal blooms (where algae grows quickly in very large numbers), which lower oxygen levels and kill fish
Toxins, such as petroleum, oil, pesticides, and heavy metals	Street runoff, industrial spills, and drains	Poisoning of animals and plants. Bioaccumulation (concentration inside living things) of poisons in the food chain. Genetic defects in animals and plants
Bacteria and viruses	Sewage and animal waste, such as dog feces	Disease. Death of animals and plants
Physical pollutants, such as plastic litter, sediment, and salt	Street runoff and drains	Plastic entangles animals. Sediment smothers river bottoms. Salt kills many freshwater species

BIODIVERSITY THREAT:
Invasive Species

Introduced species are nonnative species that are introduced into a habitat. Some introduced species become **invasive species**, spreading widely. Nonnative species may be introduced deliberately or accidentally.

Invasive Animal Species

Animal species that are introduced into a river become part of the river's ecosystem. Many species in that ecosystem are affected negatively because the introduced species compete with them for food or eats them. Introduced species are usually free of the predators and diseases of their native habitat, so they may thrive and become invasive species. However, introduced species may also benefit some native species.

Round Goby

This invasive fish from Russia is a major pest in many rivers and lakes in eastern North America. It first appeared in Canada's St. Clair River in 1990. In 2009, scientists noted large numbers of round goby in several rivers that flow into the Great Lakes of North America.

Scientists estimate that up to 90 percent of native fish species are affected by the round goby. It competes with and preys on these species, and it drives some from their feeding and breeding areas. It feeds on species on the river bottom and is a major threat to three rare freshwater mussels, called the rayed bean, snuffbox mussel, and northern rifleshell.

One positive effect of the round goby on river ecosystems is that it has become a major prey species for the endangered Lake Erie snake. One study showed that 92 percent of this snake's diet is round goby.

The round goby is an invasive river species that has both positive and negative effects on ecosystems.

Invasive Plant Species

Invasive plants can also be serious threats to river biodiversity. The table below gives some examples.

Examples of Introduced Species

SPECIES	ORIGIN	WHERE IT WAS INTRODUCED	HOW IT WAS INTRODUCED	BIODIVERSITY THREAT
Water hyacinth	Amazon River, South America	Africa	Planted as an ornamental plant in ponds	Floats on water surface and blocks light needed by underwater plants Clogs waterways
Basket willow	Europe	Australia	Planted alongside streams	Displaces native vegetation and the wildlife that depends on it
Tamarisk (salt cedar or athel pine)	Africa	United States and Australia	Planted to provide windbreaks and shade in dry areas	Displaces native vegetation and the wildlife that depends on it
Swamp stonecrop	Australia	United Kingdom	An aquarium and pond plant that escaped into the wild	Displaces riparian plants

A hippopotamus is surrounded by water hyacinth. This South American plant has become invasive in several African rivers, such as the Zambezi River.

BIODIVERSITY THREAT:
Agriculture

Agriculture depends on water and fertile soil. For thousands of years, farms have been established beside rivers, on the fertile soil of **floodplains**. Farmland has replaced huge areas of river habitat, and this has had an enormous effect on biodiversity.

Cropping and Grazing

Agriculture involves the cropping of fields and the grazing of animals. Where native vegetation is cleared right to a river's edge to make way for crops, riverbanks can become eroded. When cattle drink from a river, they trample riverside plants and make the water muddy. They may also trample the nests and eggs of freshwater turtles. When riverbanks are fenced to keep cattle away from the river, water quality improves, and riparian biodiversity increases.

Fertilizers

Fertilizers are chemicals that are used on the land to increase its fertility. Some fertilizers used on crops and pastures are washed into rivers. This causes an increase in soil nutrient levels, mainly phosphorus and nitrogen, which causes the excessive growth of algae, called an algal bloom. An algal bloom lowers the oxygen levels in a river, causing many **aquatic** species to suffocate. It can also make the water poisonous to animals. Where riverside vegetation is protected, fertilizer runoff into a river is reduced.

Crops such as taro (a root vegetable) and rice are grown on the fertile floodplains beside rivers. Clearing land to make room for these crops can damage the river habitat.

Dams

Dams are built on rivers to provide water for crops and pastures, and to generate hydroelectric power (electrical power produced by moving water). Dams interrupt natural water flows, and they restrict the movement of animals up and down a river. They can also cause cold-water pollution. This happens when water is released from the bottom of the dam wall. The water is cold and it causes the water temperature downstream to fall. Cold-water pollution can affect the breeding of many fish species.

Snag Removal

In the 1800s, in some countries, riverboats such as paddle steamers carried goods up and down rivers. These boats had wooden hulls, which could be damaged if they hit pieces of wood under the water, called snags. Fallen trees were removed from rivers so that boats could move freely. These underwater snags are important shelters and breeding places for native freshwater fish. In some places today, snags are being returned to rivers.

Australia's largest freshwater fish, the Murray cod, is affected by damming and snag removal. The Murray cod cannot breed in cold water, and it needs fallen trees and snags for shelter.

BIODIVERSITY THREAT:
Climate Change

Levels of certain gases, such as carbon dioxide, are increasing in Earth's atmosphere. These greenhouse gases trap heat, and this is causing an increase in average temperatures and climate change. Climate change affects rivers.

Climate Change in the Past

Climate change is a natural part of Earth's history. Biodiversity has changed over thousands of years as climate changes have affected and changed habitats. Today, scientists believe the rate of climate change is faster than ever. They believe that many species will have too little time to adapt to these changes and will become extinct. However, other species will benefit.

Effects of Climate Change on Rivers

Scientists are uncertain exactly how different rivers will be affected by climate change. They do know that the amount of rainfall and where it falls will change. Predicting precisely what will happen to each river is impossible, because ecosystems are very complex.

Did You Know?

Fossils of a 33-feet-long (10-m) fish-eating dinosaur have been found in the Sahara Desert, in Africa. The fossils date from 100 million years ago, when rivers flowed through the region.

As the climate changes, some areas will receive less rain and rivers may dry up, as happened to this river in Germany.

Where Rainfall Increases

In areas where rainfall increases, there may be an increase in the number of floods. Runoff of fertilizers into rivers may increase, causing algal blooms, which lower oxygen levels in the water. Riparian habitats may be washed away, increasing silt levels in rivers. Fish that hunt by sight would have difficulty finding prey.

A crocodile swims in a river covered in an algal bloom. Climate change could cause more algal blooms.

Where Rainfall Decreases

In areas where rainfall decreases, some rivers may dry out over summer months. Animal and plant species that cannot survive periods of drought may become extinct. Species that can tolerate this change may flourish. The runoff of fertilizers into rivers may be reduced, but because there is less water, their effect may be greater and cause more severe algal blooms.

Lungfish

The Australian lungfish is the only lungfish that can breathe through both its gills and lungs. It is found in slow-moving and warm rivers that have low oxygen levels. In the summer, oxygen levels fall even further. Other fish cannot get enough oxygen from the water, but the lungfish is able to take a gulp of air to breathe. This ability may mean that it is more likely to survive the effects of algal blooms and climate change.

River Conservation

Conservation is the protection, preservation, and wise use of resources. Conserving river biodiversity involves protecting it from a variety of threats. Research, education, laws, breeding programs, and replanting projects are very important to river conservation.

Research and Education

Scientific research surveys and studies are used to find information about rivers, such as how different river ecosystems work and how humans affect them. This helps people work out ways of conserving rivers. Information from scientists must be passed on to people such as students, anglers, and tourists. When people are educated about how and why rivers are important, they are more likely to help conserve them.

Breeding Programs

Some endangered river animals are bred in zoos, where they are safe from threats that could make them extinct in the wild. In North America, several species of salmon are bred in aquariums and their young are released into the wild to boost populations.

Young salmon grow in a hatchery as part of a breeding program. When they are larger, they will be released into the wild.

Replanting Projects

Healthy riparian habitats are vital to river biodiversity, and there are many projects around the world where riverbanks are being restored to their natural state. These projects involve the removal of invasive species and garbage, and the replanting of native vegetation.

Laws

Many laws have been made to protect river biodiversity. Some laws make it illegal to discharge waste water into a river or creek, and others stop people from building houses and factories close to a river. There are penalties such as fines that are given to people who break these laws.

Did You Know?

There have been more than 24,000 river conservation projects in Japan since 1990. Most of these projects were begun by local communities who decided they wanted to protect and restore local waterways.

Many riparian replanting projects are carried out by local governments or community groups.

CASE STUDY:
The Ganges River

The Ganges River in Asia flows through some of the most densely populated regions on Earth. About 450 million people live along its length, and the river's rich biodiversity is seriously threatened by human activities.

Ganges Biodiversity

The Ganges has a rich biodiversity, although many species are critically endangered because of threats caused by humans. The river has at least sixty-seven fish species, eleven freshwater turtle species, nine aquatic mammal species, and three crocodile species. It is also home to the highly endangered Ganges river dolphin.

Ganges River Dolphin

The Ganges river dolphin has a total population of about 2,000. Its low numbers are due to collisions with boats, entanglement in fishing nets, poisoning from chemical waste, and changes to its habitat. These changes include the construction of dams and diverting water for farming. More than fifty dams and barrages have been built along the Ganges. The dolphins cannot move freely, which means that different populations of dolphins cannot breed with each other. This leads to inbreeding and a loss of genetic diversity, which makes the species less able to cope with changes in its environment.

Ganges Shark

The Ganges shark is a 6.7-feet-long (2-m) species that lives in the Ganges and other Indian rivers. It is highly endangered, mainly because of overfishing.

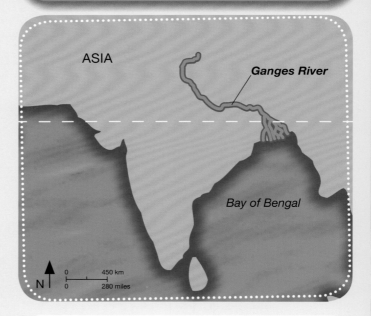

The Ganges has its source in the Himalayas mountain range. It flows for 1,560 miles (2,510 km) through India and Bangladesh before entering the sea at the Bay of Bengal.

Threats to Ganges Biodiversity

The main threat to Ganges biodiversity is the pollution that comes from the millions of humans who live alongside the river and in its catchment area.

Human Waste and Factory Waste

Every day, about 343 million gallons (1.3 billion liters) of sewage and 68.7 million gallons (260 million l) of factory waste enter the Ganges from the thirty cities, seventy towns, and thousands of villages that lie along its course. Sewage increases the number of harmful bacteria in the water. Factory chemicals can cause defects and cancers in animals and humans.

Agricultural Chemicals

Every year, 6.6 million tons (6 million metric tons) of fertilizers and 9,920 tons (9,000 metric tons) of pesticides are applied to fields beside the river. Some of these chemicals become runoff, which washes into the river. Runoff can cause algal blooms, which are poisonous to animals and reduce oxygen levels in the water.

Did You Know?

At Varanasi, a city on the Ganges, levels of *E. coli* are 120 times higher than safe levels for drinking. *E. coli* is Escherichia coli, a bacterium found in human and other animal feces. It can cause severe illness.

Hindu people bathe in the Ganges at Varanasi, a holy city in northern India. Hindus regard the river as sacred and cleansing, but the river has become very polluted by sewage and chemicals.

Climate Change and the Ganges

The **glaciers** of the Himalayas hold the third-largest volume of freshwater ice in the world, after the ice caps of Antarctica and Greenland. As the Himalayan glaciers melt, they feed the Ganges River. In recent years, the rate of melting has accelerated due to climate change. If the glaciers melt completely, the flows of many rivers, including the Ganges, will be reduced.

Inaccurate Prediction

In 2007, the Intergovernmental Panel on Climate Change predicted that the Himalayan glaciers would melt completely by 2035 due to global warming. In 2009, it was found that this prediction was based on inaccurate information. The threat to the glaciers remains, but the rate of melting is slower than first thought.

Water from the Himalayan glaciers feeds the Ganges River. If the glaciers were to melt completely and disappear, the Ganges would be severely affected.

The Living Ganges conservation project is helping to conserve the home of the Ganges river dolphin. Since the project began, dolphin numbers have increased.

Conservation of Ganges Biodiversity

The threats to biodiversity in the Ganges river system are huge. Living Ganges is a local project that was begun by the World Wildlife Fund (WWF), a conservation organization. This project began by working with local people and governments to manage a 103-mile (165-km) stretch of the Ganges in the state of Uttar Pradesh. This part of the river was chosen because it is rich in biodiversity and it has the largest population of Ganges River dolphins. If this section of river can be managed better, many species will benefit.

Living Ganges project education programs help make local people aware of threats to the river and how these threats may affect their livelihoods. The local people are then helped to reduce or remove these threats. Examples of conservation changes are:

- the banning of plastic bags in river towns near the town of Narora
- the planting of trees in some areas along the river
- the building of a sewage treatment plant.

Did You Know?

The Sundarbans mangrove forests of the Ganges delta have such rich biodiversity that they are listed as a **World Heritage Site**. Many people live in the Sundarbans. They share the forest with 500 tigers, which is the largest tiger population in India.

What Is the Future of Rivers?

Rivers are under severe threat from human activities. River biodiversity is falling, but when threats are removed this decline can be slowed or even stopped. Some species may reappear in habitats and increase biodiversity.

What Can You Do for Rivers?

You can help protect rivers in several ways.

- Find out about rivers. Why are they important and what threatens them?
- If you live beside or near a river, you can join volunteer groups who replant native vegetation in the riparian zone.
- Become a responsible consumer. Do not litter and do not waste water.
- If you are concerned about rivers in your area, or beyond, write to or e-mail your local newspaper, your state congressperson, or a local representative, and tell them your concerns. Know what you want to say, set out your argument, be sure of your facts, and ask for a reply.

Useful Websites

🖥 **http://wwf.panda.org/about_our_earth/about_freshwater/rivers**
This WWF website contains information about river habitats and rivers of the world.

🖥 **www.biodiversityhotspots.org**
This website has information about the richest and most threatened areas of biodiversity on Earth.

🖥 **www.iucnredlist.org**
The International Union for the Conservation of Nature (IUCN) Red List has information about threatened plant and animal species.

Glossary

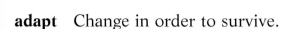

adapt   Change in order to survive.

algae (sing: alga) Simple plants without leaves.

aquatic   Relating to water.

carbon dioxide   A colorless and odorless gas produced by plants and animals.

climate   The weather conditions in a certain region over a long period of time.

current   Body of water moving in a certain direction.

delta   Large area of built-up silt where a river divides before entering the sea.

ecosystem   The living and nonliving things in a certain area and the interactions between them.

endemic species   Species found only in a particular area.

estuary   Sheltered body of water where a river meets the sea .

extinct   Having no living members.

fertile   Capable of producing lots of vegetation, possibly due to a high nutrient content.

floodplain   Area of land alongside a river that is covered when the river floods.

gene   Segment of deoxyribonucleic acid (DNA) in the cells of a living thing, which determines its characteristics.

glacier   A very large piece of ice that moves slowly across the land.

habitat   Place where animals, plants, or other living things live.

heritage   Things we inherit and pass on to future generations.

interaction   Action that is taken together or actions that affect each other.

invasive species   Nonnative species that negatively affect their new habitats.

nutrient   Substance that is used by living things for growth.

organism   Animal, plant, or other living thing.

pollutant   Harmful or poisonous human-produced substance that enters an environment, possibly causing damage to organisms.

predator   Animal that kills and eats other animals.

sewage   Human and animal waste.

silt   Soil and sediments carried in water.

species   A group of animals, plants, or other living things that share the same characteristics and can breed with one another.

urbanization   The development of towns and cities.

vegetation   Plants.

wetland   An area (not including the sea) that is permanently or temporarily covered in water.

World Heritage Site   A site that is recognized as having great international importance and that is protected by the United Nations Educational, Scientific and Cultural Organization (UNESCO).

Index